HOW TO SET UP PHOTOGRAPHY LIGHTING FOR AT HOME STUDIO

By James Christiansen

TABLE OF CONTENTS

INTRODUCTION

Photography lighting for a home studio

A truly great photo is immediately recognizable by a professional quality that is hard to define. The models glow, the product lines are crisp and sharp, and each individual family member looks their best in a portrait. Although creative flair and a high quality camera play their part, the defining feature of a great photo is how well the photographer has used the light. Great lighting can create drama and draw in the viewer, turning an ordinary photograph into true art. While the amount of new gear and techniques available can be initially daunting, creating outstanding results in a home studio is a very achievable goal for a photographer looking to take their skills to the next level. With some basic equipment, a good set-up and a trained eye, a home studio can produce images to rival established professionals.

Why is lighting important? No matter how talented the photographer or the excellence of their equipment, a photo will not be high quality unless the lighting is right. Amateurs often make the mistake of assuming that expensive equipment and complicated techniques will produce great photos. This often means that they spend the bulk of their budget on the equipment to capture a good photo, instead of the lighting which will actually create the shot. Professional studio photographers know the importance of lighting, and tend to direct the bulk of their budget to acquire high quality equipment. Using

1

natural light where possible can produced excellent images, and a detachable flash in the hands of a talented photographer is a great tool. However, even these techniques need an understanding of how light can be manipulated and directed to produce images. There are some shots that simply cannot be achieved without a studio set up to maximise the potential of lighting.

Why have a home studio?

A home studio provides a location to set up gear, and to practice manipulating the settings and surroundings to produce fantastic pictures. Taking photographs outdoors with a detachable flash or using natural light presents a number of challenges for an inexperienced photographer to combat. In a home studio, the established equipment allows the photographer to fine-tune the images they produce by eliminating variables. A home studio can be used at any time of the day and in any weather conditions, which increases the amount of hours available to work. Creating a home studio is usually a step forward towards making photography a financially viable profession. It provides a place to bring clients, and gives an air of professionalism that inspires client trust. A studio at home gives an opportunity to be surrounded by inspiring props, and to have different shooting options to hand. A home studio allows the photographer to hone their skills, and to have complete control over the set up. A large set-up fund is of course desirable, but there is a range of lighting options to suit almost any budget. With creativity and experimentation, most effects can be achieved and brilliant photos taken.

Understanding Light

Light falls into two broad categories – natural and artificial. Both have subsets; for example natural light normally refers to the sun, but it can also refer to moonlight and candle light; and they all have properties that present challenges and add unique beauty to photos. The sun in particular varies wildly in color and harshness, depending on the time of day or weather. Artificial light has unique properties, depending on the type of bulb it comes from and the accessories used with it. Photographic lights are colored differently from standard household lights to better simulate natural light.

Hard and soft lighting can dramatically impact the image – hard lighting is direct lighting that creates strong, defined shadows, while soft lighting has more of a gray area between the dark and light. The positioning of artificial light will also have an effect on the end product. Light reflected from a large surface will be soft, whereas a bare bulb will generally produce a hard light. The temperature of the color will also change based on the type of equipment being used; a candle has a warm orange light, while fluorescent lighting is bright enough to be on the blue end of the scale. Most modern DSLR cameras have features to autocorrect for white light balance, but you can research more if you choose to experiment with the manual settings.

The direction of light can drastically change your image, and most of our subconscious reactions to light direction come from how light naturally behaves. So long shadows like those produced by the afternoon sun have a tendency to appear dramatic, whereas light from below is ominous, as it is not a natural direction for light to shine. Even when a portrait looks simple, often many techniques have gone into creating the image; beauty lights to enhance the features, lights directed onto the models hair to surround the subject with a glow. Objects can absorb, reflect, or transmit light through them. In fact, it is often possible to see some of the lights used in a photo shoot as reflections in the model's eyes. While the subject will absorb the light, reflectors and light transmitters can manipulate the way the light is absorbed, therefore changing the image.

Understanding how light functions gives the photographer a chance to choose equipment to exploit favorable lighting or to compensate for an unwanted effect. With an understanding of how light can change an image, the home studio set up can be designed to take advantage of the breathtaking range that light can bring to the pictures produced there.

CHAPTER 1 – HOME STUDIO SETUP

While it may seem like a large step to dedicate a room in your house to your photography, the advantages will lift your photography to the next level. Home studios can help to relax your clients and make them comfortable, which is an excellent starting point to achieving the best photos. Having a dedicated work space enables the photographer to focus on fine-tuning their lighting techniques, and saves a great deal of dragging around the unwieldy lighting equipment from place to place.

The first consideration in choosing a room is the space available. While a large room is by no means necessary, too small a room may cause a distortion of the images. Take a few test shots to determine whether the space will be sufficient for your projects. Bear in mind that low ceilings and other features of a room will reflect light in different ways. Sound-proofing the room is essential if any video will be shot in the space, and choosing a quiet area will help to aid concentration and provide a professional work environment to present to clients. Neutral room colors work best as colored walls will reflect light tinged with these colors, and this light is difficult to correct. Leave time to adjust the studio lighting, and experiment with what works best for your space and needs.

HOW TO SET UP PHOTOGRAPHY

Creating a comfortable environment

Unless you are limiting yourself to product shots or still photography, you will need to have other people in the room while shooting. A home studio tends to be a smaller room that is loaded with lights and equipment, and temperatures can rise quickly. Some form of climate control is necessary to help clients feel comfortable, and to stop issues such as flushed cheeks, sweat patches on clothing, or shiny faces from detracting from the image. Basement studios in cold areas will need to be heated for the same comfort levels. Whether protecting from the heat or cold, some form of climate control will help to protect delicate equipment from the extremes of temperature. A home studio should have props, seating options, and other points of interest to lighten the mood when necessary. Even if the ultimate aim is for serious portraits, a few light-hearted shots can set an enjoyable tone for the shoot.

Natural light

Most rooms have windows of some sort, which let in varying degrees of natural light. While natural light has a unique effect on photographs, there should be some method available to block out the natural light to gain tighter control over the manual lights. Natural light has a simple, airy look that can be difficult to recreate with studio lights. A bright, sunny day will provide a hard light, while soft light can be achieved on cloudy days. It obviously requires less equipment to set up a photographic shoot in natural light. However, the light from the window may not be at an ideal angle, and will change from hour to hour. Fast lenses take advantage of days with less light, but they are often expensive. For all practical purposes, photography in natural light is an excellent weapon to have in the arsenal, but will not stand alone as a lighting technique. For days when the natural light will not be required, the window should be blocked off carefully. To compensate, studio lights are utilized to achieve the desired effects.

Basic equipment

The sensible approach to acquiring equipment for a home studio is to buy slowly, and build on your collection. It will be difficult to know exactly what equipment will work best for your space without practice and research. However, some pieces of equipment are fundamental to the home studio. Backdrops will need to be acquired and installed. These can range from paper models to sturdy colored vinyl. Photographers on a tight budget might consider using a carefully ironed sheet or a blank wall as a back rop. A white backdrop is essential, and it is best to keep the other choices in solid block colors such as black and navy. Do try to avoid clichéd backdrops, especially when a plain white one will help the photographer later when they are able to use photo editing software to adjust the images. Some form of tripod or stand will need to be organised to keep the camera as still as possible and perfectly positioned. For photography sessions that require the photographer to be active, consider some furniture such as a step ladder that will allow you to safely climb and achieve photos from different angles. Props are great tools for ensuring that your photos don't fall into the common trap of being repetitive. Having these basic tools will allow you to achieve the most out of your lighting and camera.

Camera settings to make the most of your studio

Settings need to be tailored to the type of shot required, the lighting that you have available and the subject of the photo. There is no one setting that will create a great photo, but an understanding of the terms can help you learn to change the settings to produce the desired image. The ISO number is a measure of light sensitivity. It originally referred to the sensitivity of a given type of film, as determined by the International Standards Organization (ISO), which it was named after. Low ISO numbers indicate the least amount of light sensitivity, while high ISO numbers are quicker, sensitive settings. High ISO film tends to be grainy. One of the most important things that a photographer can learn is how to get the best shot in different lighting conditions with the lowest possible ISO setting.

Exposure is the light recorded on the film or sensor. A picture taken in daylight with too much light on high ISO gives a glaring, unrealistic picture. On the other hand, a small aperture at low ISO and short shutter speed could make a daylight scene look dark.

Aperture and f-stop are similar terms. Aperture is the opening in the lens that lets the light through when a photo is taken. A larger aperture allows more light through. F-stop is the name that photographers use when referring to different sizes of aperture.

Shutter speed is the third part of the exposure equation. It refers to how long the shutter remains open to allow light through. Shutter speeds are given in fractions of a second: most often, shots are taken at 1/500. More motion is recorded with a longer shutter speed, which means the subject and camera need to be as still as possible. Long shutter speeds are often used at night, while short shutter speeds reduce blur, and aid in capturing images where the subject may be moving.

Studio lighting: Aims and Benefits

In many ways, taking photographs in a studio is easier than photography in other environments because it is controllable and consistent. In choosing equipment for your new studio, the first decision to make is the intended purpose for the lights. Do you have a large room that requires mobility, or can you be plugged in? Still photography only, or do you aim to take videos? Portraits or product placement? As you build your equipment and skills, you will grow more confident in different styles and methods, but it will help initially to be less ambitious. Getting a sense of your unique needs will allow you to make clear decisions on the products that are right for you.

The studio option offers tight control over lights from clearly defined sources. They offer 24 hour potential, and can be easily modified to create a desired effect. Using artificial lighting will usually show as a catch-light that appears in a subject's eyes, which can give you insight into the lighting set-up if you use professional portraits and look closely at the models' eyes. When you know what effects you want to achieve, setting up your home studio may initially take hours of experimenting before you are happy with the results. Increased understanding of the equipment and effects that are produced will come quickly, and afterwards only stylistic changes will be necessary.

Have you found this book to be helpful so far? If so, I'd really appreciate it if you can leave a review of this book by scanning this code back to Amazon.

CHAPTER 2 – CHOOSING YOUR LIGHTING

Studio lighting comes in many different forms. Many photographers will fiercely defend their preferred options, but with differing needs and tastes, there is "no one size fits all" solution.

Continuous or flash (strobe)

Continuous lights do not turn on and off with the action of the camera; the light produced stays constant throughout the shoot. They provide an even light that gives immediate feedback on how the lighting will appear in the final image without needing multiple test shots as with flash photography. The lights can be intensified or dimmed to achieve the desired effect, with instant feedback on the monitor that allows for easy fine-tuning. If the home studio is intended for video work, then flash lighting will not be suitable, and some form of continuous lighting will be necessary.

Hot lights (Halogen or tungsten lights) heat up to very high temperatures. They are effective for video lighting and for product photography. The light that they produce tends to be warm or orange in color, which will need to be adjusted with filters or other accessories if it does not work with the intended image. It can be difficult to reconcile the color with daylight or strobe lighting, as they are quite different. The ISO setting on the camera will need to be relatively high and the shutter speed quite slow to make the best use of this type of lighting. Because they get so hot and bright, they can be difficult to work with in an enclosed space, and particularly for the people involved in the shoot. Hot lights should be used with caution, as the high temperatures can cause a fire risk. They do tend to be much cheaper and more readily available, and with the right precautions should not be dismissed outright.

Cool lights are fluorescent bulbs that have a lower temperature, producing a cooler color. They mix well with sunlight, and can be used with flash bulbs. They are also effective for video, and do not present much of a fire risk due to low heat output. Cool lights will often offer some limited adjustment options through turning off bulbs, unlike hot lights, which are not usually adjustable. Continuous lighting would not provide for the entire lighting needs of most photographers, but it offers some diversity and options when trying different formats.

Flash (or strobe) lighting is the more popular choice for studio photographers, because of the increased flexibility, power, and mobility that it provides. There are two basic types: hot-shoe flashes and studio flashes. Hot-shoe flashes fit onto the "hot-shoe" of your camera. Using them while attached to the camera is convenient, but the light is direct, strong, and unflattering. However, hot-shoe flashes can be mounted on a stand and positioned around the subject to soften the effects, and can be shot through an umbrella to diffuse the light. Hot-shoe flashes are inexpensive and portable, and multiple units can be rigged up to have light coming from different directions. However, the power output is reasonably low, and test shots are the only way to gauge the results of the shoot and adjust the lighting. Hot-shoe flashes do not have adjustable power options. Most hot-shoe flashes have very short flash duration, which increases the color temperature of the flash, and creates another complication that the photographer will need to correct or adjust. A radio trigger is used to create the flash, which increases cost and decreases reliability. Hot-shoe flashes are a quick, inexpensive product to include in the studio kit, and give mobility and flexibility to the photographer. They are best suited for taking photos on the move.

Another type of flash is the ring flash. A ring flash is a ring-shaped bulb that is placed around the lens to spread light directly over the subject from all sides, eliminating shadows while maintaining the harsh light that is normally achieved using a direct flash. This method provides a more direct, larger light source, and can be used with small diffusers to soften the shadows created. The ring flash is a fairly specialised piece of equipment, used to create a certain "look". Although camera flash lighting can be used as part of a home studio lighting set-up, the best results require the photographer to diversify the types of lighting they have available.

Speedlights

A speedlight is a flash that operates faster than a regular flash, making it ideal for still or high-speed shots. As well as operating quickly, it can seem to pause motion due to the short space of time the flash is present. A speedlight has a fairly specific use, so it's worth considering whether this type of flash would see regular use in your home studio. Photonet.com offers this suggestion for a speedlight kit:

A good **small speedlight set** includes:

- **3 small speedlights:** (see On-Camera Flash vs. Off-Camera Flash)
- **3 lightweight stands**: Westcott 750 Photo Basics 7.5-Foot Light Stand, or Manfrotto 5001B 74" Nano Stand
- **2 small accessory shoe adapters**: Photoflex Light and Umbrella Shoe Mount Clamp (to hold umbrellas)
- **1 small (30-40 inch) silver reflector umbrella**: Creative Light 33" Silver Umbrella
- **1 small (20-30 inch) shoot-through umbrella**: Creative Light 33" Translucent Umbrella
- **2 small clamps**: Adorama Pro Clamp with Reversible Mounting Stud
- **Assorted filters**: Rosco Strobist 55 Piece Cinegel Filter Kit
- **2 photo eye triggers**: Wein HS Hot Shoe Slave
- 1 roll Gaffers tape

Miller, Gary. *Beginners Guide to Lighting Kits.*
March 2010. http://photo.net/learn/lighting/guide-
to-lighting-kits/beginner/ Accessed 07/20/14

Monolights

A monolight (sometimes called monobloc) is the next option up from a hotshoe flash. Reflector, power supply, umbrella, and stand, along with the AC power cord are included in a single product. They provide ease of use with their built in umbrella, radio sync slave to synchronise flashes, and ability to adjust the strength of the light. They are a good option for a home studio, as the features are created to work together and to provide a fairly fool-proof lighting solution. However, the ability to customize is limited, so a photographer wanting flexibility and the freedom to experiment should probably investigate separate studio lights.

Mains powered monolights are the most popular with people just starting out, probably because they're much less expensive than the other choices. Monolights contain all of the "works" within the flash head itself; plug them into the wall, and they're ready to go!

Studio Lights

Studio lights (known as Pack and Head lights) have a power pack, and one or more flash heads are plugged in. Pack & Head lights have many advantages over monolights, as well as being far more powerful. The pack has the controls, making it easier to access and change settings than when the controls are located high on the head. Battery-powered Pack and Head lights have increased mobility, and can be used in multiple locations where there is no option to plug the power pack into a wall socket. .

With a huge variety and range of accessories, it can be a daunting prospect to choose studio lights without a clear sense of direction. On the cheaper end of the scale and a step above the monolights are individual lights that come with inbuilt reflectors. They offer less flexibility than stand-alone units, but also less complicating features for the beginner photographer to work out. Modern flash heads can generally adjust from full to 1/16th or 1/32nd power, which is a range that is effective for most situations. Recharge time is worth considering, as less expensive models can take a long time between shots.

Some flash lighting features a "modeling lamp off" indicator, which turns the modeling light off automatically during the flash. All the flash heads should have sensors that can read when another flash has been triggered. Using a radio or infra-red trigger, the photographer fires a single flash, and the others will follow automatically. The flash heads will need to be set up in a position where they can catch the light from the trigger flash, and the trigger flash needs to be in range of the remote. Having a large power output has its advantages, but techniques such as using gels, filters, and adjusting the power settings will be needed to find the correct amount of light with minimal color shifts. A light that has an output of 300J allows the camera to be used at

100 ISO and will produce high image quality in most cases. It is better to have a more powerful light turned down, than a less powerful light constantly working to capacity and shortening its life span.

While all the choices may seem daunting, the advantage to having a home studio is that once the lights have been selected and set up, the photographer need only make minor stylistic adjustments for each shoot. A mix of lighting options is always desirable. While it may be tempting to indulge in many different lighting options at once, it is a far more effective strategy to become familiar with one or two at a time. Experimentation and experience are key factors in choosing studio lighting options and adapting them to your needs. Once the basic lighting has been chosen, there are a range of accessories and modifiers that can help bring your photography up to the next level.

CHAPTER 3 – HOW TO SET UP YOUR LIGHTING

Having made a decision on the types of lighting that suit your home studio, the next step is to consider what accessories could be used to enhance your photos. Some items can be found built in to studio lights or monolights, whereas others are far more interchangeable.

Flash head kits
Flash heads can be bought in a kit, which provides the home studio with a good starting point. Most kits have two flash heads, a flash tube, and occasionally a modelling light. Most have a "slave"remote device, enabling one flash to be triggered by another, and simplifying the remote process.

Diffusers

Diffusers work to spread light across a larger space than simply beaming the light directly onto the subject. This effect is generally achieved by passing the light through thin cloth. A bigger diffuser generally means softer shadows, so a 20-inch beauty dish will have harsher shadows than a 40-inch umbrella.

Umbrella or softbox

One of the most common studio accessories is the umbrella or brolly. Shaped much like a rain umbrella, it can be used to reflect light directly, or to pass light through and diffuse it. There are different types of

18

umbrella available, but a white shoot-through umbrella or a small silver reflective umbrella work best for a home studio environment. A soft box has a similar purpose and a comparable result. Although a soft box is more complicated to assemble, they offer greater focus and control of the light. Both spread the light out, softening shadows and lighting the whole subject. Umbrellas are usually less expensive, more versatile, and more portable. They also often come with reflective covers. The umbrella diffuses light over a wider area, whereas the soft box is better for concentrating light on a smaller area with a more sophisticated result.

Synchronising lights

All lights have to go off at the same time to effectively light the subject. There are four main options for creating this function. Hard wiring the flash heads directly is messy, and has more potential for error. Light sensitive triggers can be plugged into the sync cord, to automatically fire the flash head when it senses the primary flash go off (that is wired to the camera). Infrared triggers use infrared technology to trigger the flash. Both of these triggers tend to be sensitive to sunlight, so are best used indoors. By far the most popular method to synchronize the flashes is the radio slave, which has none of these drawbacks and effectively triggers the flash function on multiple devices.

Tripods

It is extremely disappointing to discover that a great photo has come out blurry. For a photographer wanting to experiment with new techniques, it is essential that you have a flat, solid place to stand the camera. A tripod offers perfect stability, and can be adapted for when the floor surface is not level, making it an excellent investment for a photographer who likes to leave the house.

Reflectors

Reflectors bounce light back onto the subject. In the process, the light is colored, spread out, and softened. Most reflectors are white, silver, gold, or black. There are multi-purpose kits available where one reflector can be used for all four surface colours. Sizes and shapes vary, and some experimentation will be necessary to determine what is appropriate for your work space.

Modifiers

Light modifiers can be attached to your umbrella or softbox. Modifiers can be diffusers, grids, or egg carton style. Modifiers are generally for photographers with an advanced understanding of how to use light and with a clear idea of the style they are aiming for. There are many options for modifiers to change the light. If the light is too hard, a diffuser can be added to soften it, and a grid can be added where the light is too spread out. With every change in the size, shape, or material of your diffusers, you achieve a whole new look.

Light stand

Quality stands are crucial to allow you to easily position the camera exactly where it is needed. They hold important and expensive gear, so they should be sturdy and reliable. They should allow easy and effective ways to position the lights where you want them.

Fan

Some flash heads come with a built-in cooling fan, but if yours do not you may want to consider purchasing a fan to cool them down. There is a high risk of overheating with hot lights, which at best will require you to stop mid-shoot and at worst could cause fires.

Ladder

A ladder is not an essential tool for a home studio, but it certainly is a useful one. A ladder will allow you to easily hang backdrops, take shots from up high, and will come in handy for many other small tasks.

Power options

The home studio will have a great deal of equipment requiring electricity. Be sure to stock up on extension cords so that you do not accidentally limit your movement halfway through a shoot. Surge protectors will guard your valuable items, and make sure that any battery packs have a spare on charge for an easy change over.

Modeling Lamps

A modeling lamp gives you an indication of the effect that the flash will have, rather than being intended to help light the subject. If you're using accessories like softboxes, dim modeling lights won't help you to judge the light. Some more expensive lights come pre-fitted with bright modeling lamps (at least 150 watts). Some flash heads have fixed power modeling lamps, while others feature adjustable power levels. Proportional modeling lamps can be useful, but only if they're bright enough to see with. Modeling lamps are at risk of overheating if left on for long periods of time, especially when using restrictive light shaping tools like honeycomb grids, spotlights, or snoots.

Computer programs

While most people have heard of photo-editing software such as Photoshop, it is well worth searching around to see what programs other photographers may use that would work for your home studio. In most cases, photo-editing software cannot compensate for a poorly executed photo, and it is far easier to spend a small amount of time getting the shoot right than to spend hours later editing each photo individually. With hundreds of programs available, and a wide range of prices, it is really up to the individual photographer to decide what level of editing will be necessary.

Power needs

While newcomers often adopt a "bigger is better" mindset, in fact it is important to maintain some flexibility when calculating the strength of the lights and the power needed to operate them. The power that your photo shoot will require will be based on several factors. Firstly, the shape and size of the home studio will affect the amount of light needed. Light that bounces off ceiling and walls is softened and can quickly become intense.

The quality of light created in this way is not inherently bad or good, but will need to be factored in when deciding on what the desired end product will be for the shoot. The distance from the lights to the subject will also impact the amount of power necessary to achieve the desired effect. A shorter distance will require less power, and it becomes easier to create a focused spotlight effect. Product photography and individual portraits tend to fall on this side of the power requirements. For large groups and areas, the light will need to be spread out, and more powerful equipment will be required to achieve a similar effect. In practical terms, your needs could range from 100J to 1000J or more depending on the space you have to light and the size of the subjects. Ideally, lighting that can be adjusted will save you from constantly running on maximum power and decreasing its life span, and gives you the option of more intense light or coverage of a wider area when necessary.

ISO adjustments

The type of camera and lens being used will need to be taken into consideration. Photos taken from a small lens-to-subject distance need to account for the proximity to the lighting, while photos from further away need adjustment so that the lens can pick up the same quality of light. Changing the amount of light the lens is able to receive will decrease the need to fine-tune the physical lighting. For a digital camera, changing the ISO settings will adjust the level of overall flash power. 100 ISO is a good starting point, but flash power can be "increased" if necessary by using higher ISO settings. Keep in mind that increasing the ISO settings can detract from image quality. The key is to adjust lighting to make it as close to the desired effect as possible, and then to fine-tune using the ISO settings if necessary.

With all these accessories and features, it is easy to exceed the budget on items that may not be strictly necessary. To avoid unnecessary expenditure, put a good amount of forethought into the type of room available, the type of photos you intend to take, the subjects you regularly shoot, and the effects you wish to use. Ingenuity will often serve as well as excessive expenditure. Focussing the bulk of the budget on a small amount of quality basic equipment ensures that quality photos are possible. The extras can be added over time and as experience dictates.

CHAPTER 4 – BUYING EQUIPMENT

For the beginner, there are a number of approaches to buying equipment that will depend on your budget and preferences. The idea is not to buy equipment that will create limitations, so a single piece with more adjustable functions will probably be a better investment than multiple lights that do not adjust. Second-hand gear can often be procured at low prices, as photographers upgrade their equipment or move on to different pursuits. The drawbacks to second-hand equipment are the lack of warranty, the inability to fully know the work history and storage conditions that the equipment has been subjected to, and the uncertain life expectancy of the equipment. However, as a means to obtain higher quality gear and to try different models on a budget, the second-hand route is an excellent way to set up a home studio. Even damaged pieces of equipment can often be bought and repaired for much less than the cost of purchasing them new from a retailer.

Most basic good quality lighting is durable and timeless, with some photographers using the same gear for years; although older gear may prove more difficult to match specific accessories, and you may need to come up with some creative solutions to achieve specific effects. In general however, buying good quality equipment from a trustworthy photographer is an excellent option for the budget conscious or those who would like to try new accessories without risking large amounts of cash.

Purchasing new equipment

Should you choose to purchase new equipment, consider your warranty options, and the difficulty of obtaining a replacement should you experience problems with the equipment. Buying from overseas retailers can be a cheaper option, although the security of the warranty and the expense of returning items if necessary both need to be taken into consideration. Buying from a local company that specializes in photographic lighting helps to support local enterprises, generally offers more security, and gives you the chance to discuss lighting options and preferences in person with knowledgeable sales people. It is a good idea to begin discussions with an idea of the equipment that will suit your needs, as it is all too tempting to give in to a smooth-talking salesperson, and walk out having exceeded your budget on an expensive piece where a cheaper option may have served just as well.

Researching your options

An important key is to search product reviews and get an overall sense of the quality and performance of different pieces of equipment. Each person has their own preferences and prejudices when it comes to all aspects of photography, so a key is to listen to the broad scope of feedback on a piece instead of the strongly worded negative opinion or the gushing approval of a die-hard fan. Once again, speaking to knowledgeable sales assistants can be a good tool, as they should be able to add to personal opinion with insider information on what brands are most popular, or most often returned due to faults or change of mind. Many fellow photographers would be only too happy to enter into a discussion on the equipment they choose and why.

Local photography classes and interest groups can field some interesting discussions, although it pays to ensure that you actually like someone's work before you pursue information on how they achieved it. Finally, the Internet provides many, many places where photographers from all over the world can meet to share opinions and discuss options. These photographers will not be in direct competition with you, which makes the information flow freely. Once again, a broad sense of how a product is received is more valuable than a single review which may or may not be applicable to you.

Photography Lighting Kits

Buying equipment in a kit often provides a discount, and is a good way to ensure that all equipment will work well together and covers a range of needs. Kits are put together by manufacturers or by retailers and offer a good base from which to add accessories and diversify. eBay is an excellent place to find kits that meet a wide range of needs. It is advisable to have put in a good amount of research before using a site such as eBay to find a kit. You can search by the type of kit you are looking for, the brand name of the manufacturer, or simply browse the site. Remember to check the reputation of sellers when buying over the internet. Choosing the correct kit will depend on the photographer's needs. There are kits available to suit almost any budget and need.

Do It Yourself

On the other end of the scale, some equipment can be improvised out of inexpensive products. Some photographers swear by the results they get from their extremely cheap alternatives to common lighting equipment. For example, in essence a diffuser box is just a rectangular white covering that is fitted to a lamp. It filters the harsh and direct light and diffuses it into a softer kind of light that is better for taking pictures. For objects, you can sometimes achieve the same effect by placing them into the box instead of fixing the box to the outside of the lamp.

To make a diffuser box (or soft box), untwist wire coat hangers. The pieces are worked together into a rectangular frame. To create the covering, try using the cotton from some extra large t-shirts. For a cheap solution to hot lights, aluminium reflectors with a 500-watt household tungsten bulb are often found at hardware stores and are very inexpensive. White vinyl, found at most hobby stores, provides a clean, wrinkle free backdrop. Frames to hang backdrops can easily be made using parts found at hardware stores.

DIY style lighting is quirky and imaginative. However, there are several reasons to tread very carefully in this area. Firstly, using products for purposes other than those for which they were intended can have serious safety consequences. Hot lights can be dangerous for materials that have not been made fire resistant. They can also look extremely unprofessional, and may cause clients to lose faith in your ability to produce high quality images. Basic equipment (such as back drops) has an advantage as it can be customized to fit the space it is intended for. Be sure to research carefully before investing in home-made solutions, as a professional solution may be available at a similar cost. Limiting this type of creativity to an experiment showing how a diffuser box can change a picture, for example, allows the photographer an idea of whether an investment in a high quality product is justified. Creativity is always an attribute of the best photographers, but once the budget exists for an upgrade, it may be wise to move on to more professional set-ups.

Basic Lighting Kits

eBay offers this advice for purchasing basic lighting kits:

> "There are a number of basic lighting kits on the market for the photographer just getting started. Even the basic kits range in what is included, as some may contain small camera-mounted LED lights, while others may contain larger fluorescent lights. Manufacturers like Lowel Light sell kits with a minimum of three lights, which include the main light, fill, and hair; and also offer an optional background light. More extensive kits may also include light heads, stands, frames, gels, a carrying case, and more. Because the kits themselves are available with a wide range of components, they are also priced

along a wide range. Reputable manufacturers include Lowel Light, Arri, Chimera, Dedolight, Photoflex, Smith - Victor, and Westcott.

Bowens and Westcott are among the makers of monolights and monolight kits. A standard monolight kit may include:

3 monolights, at least 150 watt-seconds each
3 light stands
2 small clamps
1 roll Gaffer's tape
1 barn door
1 reflector
1 snoot
Extension cords

Additional Lights and Accessories

As mentioned, a basic kit should include one broad source light, hair light, and a general purpose light, as well as an umbrella or softbox. When a photographer is ready to expand, there are other lights and accessories available.

Fill light
Light stands (a minimum of 4)
Extension cords
Gaffer's tape
Seamless paper background
Extra bulbs (depends on fixture)

Cloth work gloves if using halogen or tungsten lights

An assortment of colored gels and diffusion material

Clothespins for holding the gels"

eBay Guides; *How to Pick The Right Photography Lighting Kit*, June 9 2014, http://www.ebay.com/gds/How-to-Pick-the-Right-Photography-Lighting-Kit-/10000000177629043/g.html Accessed 06/20/2014

CHAPTER 5 – HOW TO EFFECTIVELY UTILIZE THE LIGHTING SET UP

With a dedicated home studio, the photographer must go well beyond a simple point and shoot tactic. While early days will be spent adjusting the lighting, eliminating shadows, and creating flattering light, it would be a missed opportunity not to delve into some of the more artistic techniques and experiment with the results. From simple portraits to dramatic high- and low-key photography, a good photographer is armed with a wealth of techniques that cater to a wide range of tastes and preferences expressed by their clients.

There are a large numbers of websites and blogs dedicated to photography techniques, and reading through these would be a great place to start. Diagrams are useful, and photos that demonstrate technique are more useful still. There is little point emulating a style that does not appeal to you (unless it's for self education or at the specific request of a client). Here are some basic techniques you might like to try to get started.

Hard and Soft Lighting

Soft light for portraits: Soft light occurs when the light finds a balance between light and dark – diffusing over the subject and creating a flattering smoothing effect. This technique can be easily achieved by firing the flash into a reflective umbrella, which evenly and softly disperses the light. Remember the hair light to visually separate the portrait from the backdrop. Most people will benefit from a soft light portrait, as it tends to bring out the best of the features of the subject.

Hard light for portraits: A modern style for fashion photography calls for hard, direct light on a subject. Generally, the light is bright, produces hard and thin shadows, and works well on subjects that don't need a soft flattering light to look good. Hard light is achieved in much the same way as other portrait photos, but all reflective umbrellas and soft boxes need to be removed. Hard light allows the photographer to play with shadows. Be careful that shadows flatter the subject by enhancing contours and creating a "3D" effect, as well as creating more interest in the image. Hard light portraits work well as Low Key images, and are often striking when presented in black and white.

Techniques to Try

Basic Portrait Light: This set-up uses two softboxes: a small one below and a large one above it, at the same angle. The large softbox acts as the key light, and it could be used to light the background. The small softbox acts as the fill light. The photographer would shoot right through the gap in the vertical axis between the softboxes, while standing behind them. The two soft boxes light the subject's face from different angles, and fill in any deep shadows while bathing them in flattering light.

Basic Fashion light: This set-up uses a 4x6 softbox with a grid, and a reflector. You can move the reflector closer to the model for more fill, or further away from the model for less fill.

Basic Beauty light: This set-up is exactly the same as the fashion light set-up above, with a beauty dish instead of the large softbox. This directs the light and creates greater contrast.

Lens Flare Effect: This set-up uses a ring flash above and to one side of the model, and a bare head behind the model on the same side for some intentional lens flare.

High key photography – High key photography has exposure set to very high levels, with the lights set to almost completely eliminate shadows. The predominate shade is white, and is used to convey a happy or pure tone. These images have a distinct lack of contrast. The high key photographer must be careful not to overexpose and lose the focal point for the image.

Low key photography – Low key photography uses very high contrast with dark tones. Light is used only to show the contours of the subject. Low key photography tends to convey serious or sad tones, with deep, powerful images.

Whatever lighting options you choose, have fun with them and spend time experimenting. Practice setting up multiple lights in different configurations. Practice reflecting light off different objects, using umbrellas, the walls, and the ceiling. Practice using different types of lighting, such as hair and background lights. You'll find that with an understanding of how light works, even the simplest lighting set-ups can produce striking images. Research is extremely important and with so many resources available, search for images and styles that you enjoy or would like to replicate. It's important to try new things. Even if a particular style will not be a focus of your work, it helps all aspects of your photography and increases your general knowledge on how to use lighting to good effect. Do not simply put up your lights in the same way each time - experimentation will yield surprising results. Put the lights in different positions – higher than usual, to one side, using different filters. Make your investment in lighting gear worthwhile by practising with it and then using it in all the creative new ways you discover.

CONCLUSION

Creating a home studio can initially be a daunting prospect, but you will soon learn that it is a very achievable goal. Even a modest sized space will normally be sufficient. Lighting your studio means carefully considering your goals and choosing your equipment wisely. Your final aim should be to have many different types of lighting and accessories that you can utilize when necessary. However, initially you should choose carefully and thoughtfully, with a focus on the type of images that you would like to produce. There are multiple places to buy equipment – from specialized retailers to second hand sites. Research is key, and learning from the experiences of others will enable you to avoid their mistakes and head directly for the products that are likely to produce the best results. Once you have your kit assembled in your new home studio, it is important to spend as much time as possible experimenting with different techniques. There are literally thousands of books and online courses that can be accessed for little or no cost, and that will help you break out of the mold and try new effects with your studio lighting. Remember to practice and be creative, and you will be well on your way to producing breath-taking photographic images.

I truly hope that hits book has given you a great start to getting your own home studio lighted properly, and if so, I'd really appreciate it if you can leave a review of this book by scanning this code back to Amazon.

I also love to connect with my readers, so please feel free to follow me on Twitter @JChristBooks or email me at the9cygul@gmail.com

ADDITIONAL RESOURCES

Video Resources

These videos are hosted on the educational website Udemy, an easy-to-use platform for online learning. All of these videos are taught by experts and, after reading this book, they can augment your learning and teach you even more great ideas.

Digital Photography: An Introduction to Lighting
Christine Lee Smith

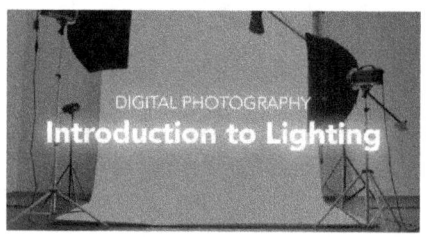 

Course Description
If you're anything like I was when I started photographing professionally nearly 10-years ago, you're intimidated to try out external lighting for your photography. I almost let fear win, but then I learned: "It's just light."
In this course I will help you transform your understanding and thinking about lighting for your photography through video lectures, images reviews, course downloads, and assignments throughout designed to integrate your learning.

Students will walk through the course by covering the basic types and qualities of lighting, including sample photos of each along the way.

Designed to be complete over the weekend you can complete the course as fast or slow as you like - while working on your lighting knowledge and skills independently in between sections.

Take this course if you want to free yourself of the fear of lighting, or if you're looking to incorporate something new and exciting in your photography! Liberate yourself and take advantage of all that photography has to offer through learning about lighting's options, uses, and functions

Chasing the Light: Photography and the Practice of Seeing

Peachpit Press

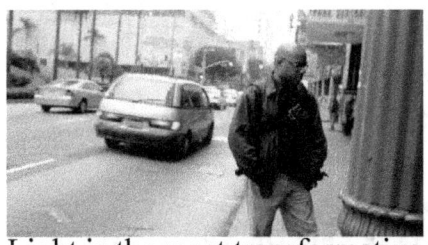 

Light is the most transformative tool at any photographer's disposal. Whether the lens is turned on people, wildlife or landscapes, the creative use of light can make the difference between a snapshot and a powerful photograph. This "Lighting in Photography: Learn Photography Lighting Techniques" video course provides a look into one photographer's approach to seeing and using available light. Ibarionex Perello, author

39

of the acclaimed book Chasing the Light: Improving Your Photography with Available Light, takes you on a visual journey through the streets of Los Angeles, not only explaining his approach to creating great street photography but also teaching you how to develop your own way of seeing. You experience shooting over his shoulder as he explains how to effectively capture light, shadow, and color, and how to approach strangers for street portraits. This "Lighting in Photography" video will inspire and empower you to overcome the obstacles that can stand in the way of your creativity.

Sign up for this Lighting in Photography course right now and learn exclusive photography lighting techniques.

Written Resources

Here are five books suggestions for further reading on the subject of lighting. Online book buying sites such as amazon.com have the advantage of offering reviews and access to second-hand copies. If you are not ready to commit to buying a hard copy, consider researching at the library or downloading the eBook version where available.

The Studio Photographer's Lighting Bible by Calvey Taylor-Haw

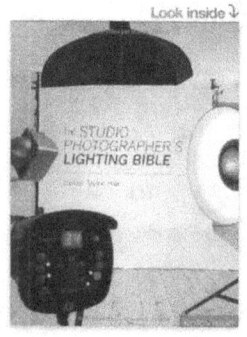

Lighting is a fundamental concern for the studio photographer, and The Studio Photographer's Lighting Bible explores lighting from every angle. This book explains all the commercial, practical, technical, and creative issues to identify how studio photographers can work successfully with other professionals and make the best and most creative lighting choices in their work. Interviews with lighting specialists from other disciplines give the photographer innovative ideas and the understanding needed to work as part of a team. The Studio Photographer's Lighting Bible is a must-have for every working photographer.

Light It, Shoot It, Retouch It: Learn Step by Step How to Go from Empty Studio to Finished Image by Scott Kelby

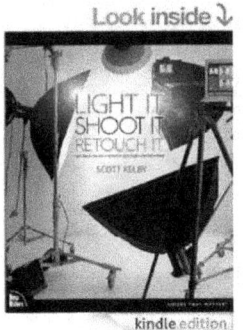

From the well-known photography blogger Scott Kelby comes this in-depth look into the process of creating spectacular images from start to finish. The book features many photos and detailed explanations of how photography techniques can be achieved. Bring your images up to the next level and learn new ways to use your gear from this illustrated guide.

Online Resources

Any photography sites recommended can only be a starting point for any photographer interested in learning. Having said that, here are 5 distinct and informative sites to begin your search.

http://photonhead.com/ Photonhead is a beginner's guide to all aspects of photography and an excellent resource for refreshing your existing knowledge and gaining some new tips.

www.photo.net has a wide range of photography resources, including a forum dedicated to lighting where you can discuss your questions and concerns with other enthusiasts and professionals.

http://www.dpreview.com/ Digital Photography Review is a single location with a wealth of information. Products, techniques, and manufacturers are reviewed with a comments section for people to express their personal experiences.

www.photoflex.com – The Photoflex website offers a wide range of products to browse through as well as some tutorials and tips. This website is worth looking at for inspiration and to see what types of products are available. Be sure to use this website only as a starting point and branch out.

http://photosecrets.com/ Photosecrets is primarily a travel photography website, but loaded with tips and tricks for any photographers. A beautiful site to inspire and instruct.

Disclaimer

All attempts have been made to verify the information contained in this book but the author and publisher do not bear any responsibility for errors or omissions. Any perceived negative connotation of any individual, group, or company is purely unintentional. Furthermore, this book is intended as entertainment only and as such, any and all responsibility for actions taken upon reading this book lies with the reader alone and not with the author or publisher. The reader alone holds sole responsibility for any consequences of any actions taken or not taken after reading this book. Additionally, it is the reader's responsibility alone and not the author's or publisher's to ensure that all applicable laws and regulations for business practice are adhered to. Lastly, I sometimes utilize affiliate links in the content of this book and as such, if you make a purchase through these links, I will gain a small commission.

www.ingramcontent.com/pod-product-compliance
Lightning Source LLC
Chambersburg PA
CBHW071244220526
45468CB00002B/999